1973

1973

Rob Nixon

Copyright ©2020 Rob Nixon
All rights reserved
ISBN-13: 978-1-7327842-9-1
September 2020

1973

Cubs

I've seen the young cubs
navigate their way.
Much stronger ones are there too,
in the way.
Time to leave the woods.

The Treatment

What will the instinct be translated into?
How will it be publicly released?
Oh, look for facts!

Professor Plum

I have failed in instructing the youth.
They are wearing bow ties and going to the office.
They don't attend meetings!
They've all gotten married.
I was one of the ones in charge of that apparently.
The silent verdict and action will be to ignore me.
It will be terrible.

Ghost Story

He disappeared,
right before the trigger squeezed,
in that instant,
the gunman saw it.
It was videotaped.
After he told us he saw it,

he waited for the footage,
he didn't say anything more.
And the tape confirmed it.
Alex moved thirty feet to the next row of cubicles,
a move that normally would have taken five seconds,
he did this instantly.

QuickCam

The case remained open, not talked about.
Five years ago,
an old webcam angle opened up.
Carole Johnson had an operating webcam right there.
She would definitely have that area in view.
It was thoroughly investigated at the time and determined
to be off at the time and that no images were captured.
That was in 2000.
In 2015, an acquaintance of hers
was arrested on voyeurism charges.
The man had several operating
cameras installed throughout Ms. Johnson's condominium.
He was also quite the computer wizard.
There was only footage beginning from 2002
discovered among the remains.
(The man committed suicide.)
We assigned our best wiretap surveillance guys to it,
and they've been working on it ever since.
Today they emailed me they found something.

Instances

1973

He ducked,
swooped more like,
pounced—
head down, and three cubicles down around the corner,
and then back up, dusting and walking along
as if nothing happened.
He ducked!

Massage

Each part is sectioned off
and is molded into a beautiful form,
then it is released gently
back into its original form,
then molded beautiful again.
Each section gets this treatment several times.

Exile

Groups excommunicate,
bullies take over groups.
When this association is taken away,
there is extreme anxiety.
Does being alone make this unbearable?
Yes.

Where?

Most people traveled because they had to,
it was part of their job,
or something else of that sort, a fugitive.

There are major cities on the east coast
within very easy travel distance.
We'll have to move to the east coast.

Medication

Find a nice partner and live together.
This brings other mental disorders,
but as long as things remain amiable,
the anxiety we're talking about is under control.

Spotless Interior

I just hear the rhythm and tone of the words going on.
I could respond appropriately if called upon,
I fit into this.
I have posture and manners too!

Raw

I like imagining we are this age,
that this thing we live on is the world,
and that things will end.
I like experiencing that with you.

Separated

I am here
and where I was rejected
at the same time.
I am here and hate it.

1973

Fear of Success

As a gift,
when success does come,
I am allowed to direct things for a while.
I think the fear is of me.

Check

I have nothing to do with reality.
I mostly concern myself
with corrupting the past and future.
Logic and all the emotional nonsense rule the present.

Calendar

Music, as always, is pouring in.
There is lots of wine as usual too.
And with a glazed eye,
and cocked head,
I will figure out my schedule.
I have a lot of planning to do.
I am the subject of these events.
Better than being the subject of the music.
That would be crazy.

Windows Shopping

I look fabulous in these.
I wear round glasses because they look great—
purple frames!

Mixed Message

"This is my alone time."
He handed me this note without a word,
and left the room.

Bottom Line

I will shop in this place again,
she is really nice,
they have my business.
What is going on in the backroom?
I don't care.
Who owns this place?
It doesn't matter,
there is nice stuff and she is nice.

Stain

It is social conditioning,
and a critical mass type thing,
this organism is insane.

Attention

I see the public defender calmly listening to my
Kennedy conspiracy theory.
When I was in his position,
I tried to be sympathetic too,
a listener.
I think part of that is logical,
not engage an expert in their field of expertise.

The other part is fear.

Nonsense

Nonsense engages me.
I am enraptured,
I am totally filled up by it.
It's amazing,
it's just nonsense.

Commence

I have figured that this is part of the plan,
entering into my delusions.
A way in at least, right?

Base Prayer

This has nothing to do with the spikes of love and hate.
Those two things cannot be engaged.
This totally has to do with the way
I navigate through reality,
my behavior during normal times.

Spikes

The ape on the tree limb is studying on things.
He immediately see you've engaged repulsion.

It Is My Business

Why has this gotten confrontational?

Because you are wrong.
You are part of the critical mass.

I Forgot to Mention

I knew it wasn't in my best interest to counterpoint
bigfoot, ghosts, aliens, or whatever,
but I did it,
I did it all the time.

Avoidance

The present is a 250 pound linebacker
to the ribs at full speed.
That microsecond
expanded to a full ten minutes or whatever.
I am usually very quiet,
subservient,
nodding.

Psyche

She is in this head too.
She is a full partner in the present.
Think of it as a clinical intervention.

Friendship

Brian Urlacher full speed at his peak.
I think this will go on for months.
I will try to remain as silent as possible.

1973

I want the impulses of this to go into my bones.

Party Member

The excommunicated will look and sound
more like members than they used to.
I'm not part of the group, but…
They have that dynamic going on.

Viral Thinking

Every time I open my mouth I infect.
I have to isolate myself.
Those I talk have to talk with,
I don't know, some may survive.

Steady

You will not end up with Annie Hall.
It will be with someone never mixed up in things.
It won't be the opposite though, no one born on a compound.
It will be someone old,
someone marginalized,
someone ugly.

Artistic Roundtable

It's hard to look at positively,
but the fact that people I can't stand
are the ones who've created the most sublime, inspired
works of my lifetime,

can be looked at as an open door.

A Laugh and a Dismissal

The ordinary given psychotic interpretation,
this is the new meditation.
It's loud, obnoxious, listens to rock music,
and watches television.

Empty More

The real person that forced me to do that stupid thing,
and that real person,
and that thing,
and so on,
I was conditioned, I am conditioned.
But I am alone now.
I am going to have to take that job myself.
All those people, I'll have to replace all those people!

Mary Tyler Moore

I am going to walk around the lake,
and watch joggers go by.

Bionic

Keep my ear open for the BS,
and kick ass as necessary.

Enlarged

One amongst others in a habitat?
Not for long.
I am two.

Perfect Faith

I believe things are going my way.
There is an absence of actual evidence on this.

Lithium-Ion Battery

This thing inside me not only pollutes my interior,
it gets into the atmosphere.
It is settling into the lungs of those around me,
and it is changing their behavior.

Ratings Book

Red throughout,
every single row.
The ones less than 10% stand out.
A second book comes out.
Still red, even redder,
plus/minus is always minus,
every single one.

Untouchables

Then the poets come in
because no action is taken,
no personnel changes,

nothing is done at all.

Come on In

The sweet, kind encouraging words,
and the flattering of my intelligence,
does help me to fold away into your presence,
I will give you that.

Diagnoses

Having confidence that things will turn around is sadness,
lost is depression.

Wary

I think I am being tricked into reacting,
that I am being purposely triggered.
Not reacting keeps the original suspicion alive,
it never goes anywhere,
it is always there.

Feelings App

I fill in the blanks,
question 4, yes,
7 through 9, yes, yes, yes,
and,
now the graph—
it looks like a dance step diagram!
Check out the Bowie cover!

Arbitrary Constant

They make some difficult question,
a question embedded in the middle of everything,
the key question for advancement.
All responses from all applicants thenceforth
are measured relative to that first test and its answer.
That gives the new numbers at least some meaning.

Mithras

Soldiers, sailors, they traveled,
they knew the gods.
The gods were invoked in contracts.
He would be perfect for treaties.

The Motions

I see the same last names
and known family connections
are dominating.

Emotions

Since we are all capable of something,
fiction should be able to proceed as if we are,
at least temporarily.

Doer

Having followers,
people who believe I am producing inspired works,

unnerves me.
On the one hand, I agree with them,
I wouldn't do what I do
if I didn't believe that myself.
On the other,
I don't think people should make such a fuss about it.

Summer

The valley kept some of the water,
the rest dried out.
Grass started growing up all around it
down there,
but the summer has turned it all brown.
The pond is absorbing more of the surrounding water
as it itself streams it away
to make clouds
somewhere else.
90°, 90°, 90°, day after day,
the ground cracks,
breaks,
absolutely dies.
The deeper wells are seeping away now.
The sky is taking everything.

Job

The scholastics fit into their comfy consolation prizes,
into their recliners,
their undoubted intelligence now commercial,
now cashed in,

three hours a day, three days a week.

Employment

We are going to have to find a way
to make this mandatory.
People are reacting negatively to this passive aggression.

Eyewitness News

That is the way to make people think, public executions.
They have really good interrogation techniques.

Message Boards

The fractured phrases that don't really seem to go anywhere,
a prologue or an afterthought can connect them up.

The Unintended This

It is the thin shell of the present tense and life,
and it has only sadness in it.
The rest is logical—no change is possible.

The Intended That

Stuck in some backward reality,
unable to cope when this is challenged,
and committing atrocities as a result.

Back Row

The cleaned and pressed greet and welcome,
they are beautiful.
Now, the back row,
they all look at me,
they are anxious—
they are me!
Everyone else is me!

Front Row

Among the first order, there is competition.
They compete to understand the new technology,
the new style.
Quickness is key here,
you can't be middle-aged.

Day Visitor

It's a graduation ceremony,
a ceremony that lasts for years.
No wonder there's angst.
All my lessons learned.
I hope they were true.
I just feel changed,
changed into.

Night Visitor

The smell of leather cleaner
heavy
coats the room.

How to enter without getting wet?

The Goods

The goal is a positive statement in support.
This is usually a negative statement against something else,
we can't get enough of that.
Argument, force, and bribery in their 21st century forms utilized
in order to get the agreement signed.
Most have buyer's remorse.
I sign with my left hand.

Buyer's Remorse

This is where the real fraud is.
You didn't buy anything!
These *promises* to repay have been around forever.
There is nothing to repay!

Anthem

The rock and roll studios
pump out the subliminals.
The brooding rock and rollers
repeat the same lines over and over.
Some use the F word,
they say join the cause,
free the people,
your way is dumb,
sex is the reward.

Pop

Others sing about medication,
the expensive street medication,
groove and be silent,
I am weak and you are strong.

Him

Then the cleverest of the weasels comes out.
He does not like religion,
and it is target practice,
behind the back,
over the shoulder,
a pirouette and a bow.

Steel Bars Bang Down

The tough guys are the bullies of the yard,
they don't wear shirts.

Ana Ng

She is given the government post,
she is in power,
she is a Levitical name in a list of one hundred,
she is a brick in a pyramid.

Importance

The fake, play-acting for approval isn't really that,
there is an outdoing spirit behind it,

at least for a second or two—
I am better than you.

Resource

Why muck things up by requesting an adjustment?
A compulsion to give back an overpayment
just takes productivity time away
from staff trying to provide
a product or service
to consumers.

Faces

There are more than one.
We have a frontal lobe, it organizes them.
It does this so we can all get along,
and get thing done.

Rush Hour

I hear something similar was found in Tanzania.
Nothing like this though, there are thousands here.
They were going somewhere when they died,
they were in their cars,
knives and guns in between their leg bones,
hair in pretty decent shape—
wouldn't they have finally just walked out?
They were definitely in a traffic jam,
almost all the cars are touching.
Interesting gaps of gravity and momentum,

they came to a rest, that's the translated name
in Tanzania.

Archeology

A Volkswagen Jetta,
six bags in two mixed stacks in the back,
two females in the front, two guns.
Enough bodies have been studied,
these bags are gold.

Realsimple.com

Glasses and contact lenses,
slippers,
sunglasses,
gloves or mittens,
heavy sweaters,
long underwear,
neck warmer or scarf,
snow boots,
turtlenecks,
warm hats,
waterproof ski jacket,
waterproof ski pants,
waterproof socks,
batteries for small electronics,
camera,
electronics chargers,
hair dryer,
poles,

1973

ski bag,
ski boots,
ski goggles,
ski lock,
skis,
antibacterial wipes,
body lotion,
comb and brush,
contact lens solution,
deodorant,
face cleanser,
first aid kit, including gas-relief tablets,
antacid,
antidiarrheal medicine,
antihistamine for allergies,
bandages,
mild laxative,
non-aspirin pain reliever,
thermometer in a hard case,
floss,
lip balm,
moisturizer,
personal-hygiene items,
prescriptions,
shampoo and conditioner,
soap,
sunscreen,
toothbrush,
toothpaste.

Mathematical

He said that he gets right down into the computer logic.
He applies for things online that are really complicated,
things that involve dozens of pages
and a progress bar on top *25% completed*,
things that involve bank accounts.
Someone asked if he keeps on *auto complete*,
surprisingly he said yes.
He tries
really hard
to understand each question,
and answer them correctly,
even if they are detrimental to his application.

Jason's Seminar

He refers to Seattle as a person.
It's all very messianic and biblical,
Book of Revelation type stuff,
that is my vibe on it anyway.
But Beckie is enraptured.

Bourgeoisie

Dumping the ones you need,
coddling and being disrespected by the ones you keep.
Workplace behavior policies being violated all the time,
and nothing's done about it.
Productivity is at an all-time low.

1973

Surrounded

I see emails from the before-time.
Things were so different then.
The subject lines are ridiculous.
I don't read any of them.

Basics

The plan is not working.
I have to come up with a new one.
I have to move to a new city and reinvent myself.
That sounds so stupid.
Get a unique hobby that will take up all my time.
That sounds even more stupid.
I will have to find new friends,
ones who won't make my skin crawl.
Go to lots of parties—
but normal people don't go to parties anymore.
Shit!
The hobby will have to have events, lots of them.

Mistake

The missionaries zigzag the neighborhood.
They do it in perfect grid patterns and symmetrical shapes.
They are dressed in shirts and ties.
They ride bikes and smile at everyone.
I will not answer the door when they come.
I sit down cross-legged, my back against the door—
knock, knock, knock.

Please go away—
knock, knock, knock.
I want to fix dinner—
knock, knock, knock.
I hear the bicycle chains rattle a bit
and the clicking of the wheels,
they are going away.
I get up,
and my fists clench.

The Chronic

Mistakes in life and hard scenes in movies
point things into fists all the time.
There is a *I can't change this* about them.

Squeeze

Every company we hated were represented in that kitchen.
Nabisco, General Foods, Kellogg's,
they all seem to smile at us.
The conversation, that I was not a part of,
was all just names mostly,
name after name,
and numbers,
numbers, numbers, numbers.
I was here, I didn't need to be counted.
Cartoons blared from the living room,
kids screeching,
and TV pitchmen,
I heard them instead.

I asked if I needed a gun.
Everyone around said "no", and "I don't think so,"
you said "yes".

Dark Room

Surprise requires a new word in the dark.
Suddenly becoming aware of something
before shutting your eyes
and shutting them hard.

Blackmail

It's a list of all the websites,
pages and pages of them.
And GPS tracking of all the physical addresses,
all the places I've visited.
My photos are attached.
I don't remember any of it.

Agitate

Do get yourself lost in the smelly stacks,
write yourself into the vast unread.
Maybe you can con your way into a tenure.
Be sure to surround yourself in renaissance art,
and have fresh oranges in your office.

Public

Seal yourself into a perfect bureaucracy,

all the time making the problems worse,
all the time worse and demanding more funds.

Store

Even before the blacklist started,
and its inevitable backlash,
I was being outsold,
and it was by a substantial margin.

Bias

I can say
that I'm not unfairly judging the artistic quality,
I can say that all I want,
but I don't like the artistic quality
because of the message,
I can't get past it.

Thud

I am inspired to respond,
and the product falls flat.

Inevitable

I won't recognize their faces,
they will be maniacal.
Will I die well?
Be murdered well?
It seems to matter.

God, it's going to hurt so bad!

Reflection

I don't see people around him mistreating him,
shaking their heads,
laughing at him.
Just details—hair, teeth.
That it's me just doesn't enter into it.

Reception

The sound is off.
I turn it up.
And it *is* me talking.
This is going to be harder to explain.

Segment

It is a story, it is a sales pitch, it is my religion.
Put on more makeup next time.
I really should think about better lighting too.

Conversion

I'm still going to think that.
I don't know what you're accomplishing.

America's Funniest Home Videos

The entire world on a deck,
and the deck collapses.

Not the aftermath,
not the bones,
the shock of it collapsing,
the sudden fall,
planetary.

Loner

No, I won't assimilate.
I will not make mistakes.
I will do things quietly
in my office.

Economics 101

Bold glasses, visible tattoos,
appeals, begging,
Microsoft Teams—the application logs my disconnection.

Red

Folded away, folded away,
many times over,
taxes and fees at targeted levels,
immediate capital—
we can still pick'em clean.

Redder

This is going to be a tribute,
an ongoing thing,

more percentage, more percentage.
Anemia will set in,
sectors will shut down,
fault lines will break.

Misery Index

The little guy copes. He puts on sunglasses,
goes out to his car and drives to the next place.
There is a lot of sadness in that car.

Levelers

The better part of leaving is oppression.
The weaker accepts the inevitable, awaits the chance.
It's not hard to understand—getting away from pain.

Press Release

If you must know,
we don't really have much in common,
we just get together as much as possible
and fuck.

Prophet

I'm not criticizing a medical treatment plan.
I'm not mass prescribing something different.
You're the brave one, doctor, not me.

Tongues

There's always the sing-songiness to the words.
That's the invisible part.
It gets lost in the translation,
but it can be put back together
in a new way.

Guerrilla Art

As we get older, we're less likely to appreciate
a clever, skewed view of things.
Guilty.
Say something aggressive that agrees with my politics,
say it with tattoos and accessories,
that is my idea of clever and skewed.
I will piss all my money away on that.

Continuing

If you've somehow convinced yourself
to feel bad about this,
I don't feel guilty about it at all.
I do feel fear,
because of the violence and everything,
but I sleep fine at night.

Wind Wind

It whirls up inside of me,
banking hard,
roaring.
I don't have the self-control

or wisdom
to let it loose at night
or in my bones.
Talking is the way it is released.
I do it in the third person.
It is never a you and me thing.
If it were,
I would be healthier mentally,
but probably not physically.

Push

All that will be left will be the ancillary,
the ones protecting what's going on,
and the ones training.
No one sane wants to be in charge of anything,
no one listens to them.

Pull

Packs get warrants and steal goods.
They've learned to sell them,
then they disappear.

Dark Life

Twilight night,
getting colder,
neon music heard interior,
rush hour traffic a half a mile away,
no one is loitering,

millions of cars at stoplights,
millions of people crossing.

Circus

If you can make me laugh,
I will be your friend, wink.
I don't completely trust my taste in other things.
And it's just for laughs,
that makes disappointment less acute.

My Scene

I study from the outside,
and understand the depth,
understand the plan.
A higher form built this.

My Seeing

On the inside,
the signs make sense.

Square

There is a safe place to go.
I don't care how many times I have to visit.
My thoughts are organized there.
The shape of the room demands I respond appropriately.

Forgetting

1973

Younger, I was preoccupied with fitting in,
and my bones were invested in absorbing things.
If I had gone to college,
my bones would have gone to parties.
Contributing to the world is in my bones now.

At Hand

I will remove the clutter.
I will get things organized.
Nonsense is in the past.
I am responsible.
I am a consultant.

Desensitization

The contemplative sitting across from each other,
the wooden chairs,
the encountering each other's humanity,
tick-tock—
this initiates my irritation protocol.
You are malnourished,
you have wrinkles,
gravity is sagging you,
your hair is unappealing,
what is that smell?

A Bar

I see *not disappointed anymore* glint across your face.
Won't we both come back here again?

There is no our place.
Why not make it this one?

Witness

I do try to please the strong ones.
Since that is everyone,
a general theory of what is right and wrong has developed.
It is not just a military man,
a corporate executive,
a self-help guru,
my brain won't be trained in on any one of them.

Mettle Detector

Chromosomal time bombs are dropped into
the population all the time.
My parental instincts are always triggered,
even when I was five—
I will show you what is good and bad.

Nazirite

He will see that side of it,
not just the ideal.
The ideal is eternal,
those who serve the offices are not.

Shiva

He speaks out a contagion.

The mind cannot be convinced another way.
I cannot be convinced.
I breathe in your transmissions.

Brahman

The dying take their surplus of atoms up into the brain,
then drop them out into the atmosphere.
Atomic processes are going on,
linking up and releasing.
I am absorbing,
building up.

Exorcist

The assassination attempts
fail as long as I want them to.
These things are exciting!
I like being in the holy land!

Heaven's Gate

When your mission was over, Do,
when you were asked your findings on the humans,
you just listed their faults,
how clueless they all were.
Right, smelly humans, yawn.
You were given a quality vehicle,
and every chance in the world.
Your mission has been an abject failure, my friend.
All the years of Mr. and Mrs. Soft-tones,

the air purifiers,
the same meals every day,
all the years of it just seemed like
something to be skipped over to find a point,
and there was none!
We'll get something out of this, don't worry,
your crew was very interesting.

Cine

You know those pictures?
Those old, old pictures?
Weird clumps of hair
growing out of weird clumps of face.

Channel 10

This is Brother Warren, that is Brother Josh, he sings too.
I'm glad you stopped by.
I don't talk about my Christian life much—surprise!

Hurricane Jeannie

What did I think back then?
I thought some amazing things.
There was a more messianic quality to it.
It was totality back then too.
Every single song,
every single television show,
they were all connected,
like that *Beautiful Mind* guy,

all tied together with yarn.

Sometimes

Well, I watch things and listen to things that interest me.
It's natural I would tend to represent myself,
in the things that entertain me.
Say a prayer and cast the net,
gather it up and all the fish are there.

Sense Us

Fire a round off
about an hour after dark.
It's worth the ammo.

Breather

You were watching me?
You can't do that!
And it's still going on?
You can't stop!

I Feel It So

You're so many.
I don't feel surrounded.
I guess I do.

A Social

I don't think I have it in my jeans

to dive into the barbeque, bare-chested.
Backyard set?
No, no, no, no,
not now, not ever.
I don't wear boots,
have hair that falls right,
or carry weapons.

Hottie

The new aristocracy wants to fight.
They always want to fight,
take things.
All the *takey* things they learn very well.
Then they start.

Nottie

I am not an explainer.
This is what you wanted and this is what you got.
A thread goes through this rambling, several of them.

You Get It

You see it all, don't you?
How each angle tends into each another,
how it all works?
If you don't, so some research, you will learn.

A Peal

1973

Sure, it's happened a second time,
but the long gap leaves off the possibility
of this being some other kind of objective reality.
It's not a *Twilight Zone* repeating hell.
That would be the dumbest kind of hell ever!
Repeating itself every 25 years?

Ad Men

The new ones are quitting, and it's not because of money.
Management believes it's because of money.
They back this up with real statistics.
I cannot refute them.
Many of them have indeed gone on to make
tons of money in advertising in other agencies,
but that is not what made them quit.

Collectors

Nobody's watching,
nobody's reading,
the funds are now arm-twisted.
Investment goes mostly into this talent.

Brass

The practical ones in the army
just want any kind of religion to fortify the civilians.
It can even be spaced out into different denominations.
It gets creepy when it's any more than that.

Derrick

This is a geyser.
The thought of putting a lid on it does not occur.

Pumping

When it comes to things like this—
I mean, you can't get more mental and physical, right?
Maybe killing and battery, but that's way out of bounds.
Not much remaining except this to get to know one another.

Dreck

Paying money to dominate,
and a great falling away.
The *done all time*
with added originality
can only be tolerated
for as long as it takes to find *next*.

Community

It just seems everyone who likes it
has their job depending on it.
It's all just a pretend artistic industry,
and fake people within it.

Exercise

I walk my way on out of it,
visit another street in insanity,

go down those back alleys.
It's nice here,
regular people enjoy my description of things.
True, there are those of you who object to my being here,
I will just use the rear service-doors,
you won't even notice me.

This City

It's already happened here.
There are competent people at the top,
but they only do what the bullies want.
Then everyone pretends up a positive
attitude about everything!
Shit!

Bedroom Community

On money matters, I am a total dub.
And does that ever impress the chicks!
Not really caring much—no check that—
having learned not to care about it,
it doesn't bring me down.
I don't denigrate it.
I think it's a real cool skill to have.
Hey, I might learn the ropes someday.
As for now, it seems pointless.

Invisible

I won't dignify that with a response.

I'm on the outside
looking in.
You know that.

Blaise

The full-blown electrical experience was real,
but it was the integration of all circuits,
central and peripheral,
total physical and mental awareness,
not fire.

Conversation

I thought I would be treated fairly here.
I'm not a real person if I'm not hated,
at least part of the time.
I like binocular vision.

Real Conversion

You know how sometimes that shiver goes through you?
That times a lot—buzz—
just for a second or two.

At First

I had that panic attack,
then another.
Talk about your guerrilla art!
Did I?

I don't remember.
I may have.
I was definitely capable.

At Last

It's not understandable,
but that last nerve fiber in my left little toe
is under my direct cerebral control.
I do things at the right time,
all the nerves and muscles are on board,
that is an established fact.
Will they transmit outside the body?
Shoot it out forward, face to face?
Shoot it out sideways, all around?
Flood the world?

Stay in the Car

Outside, walking around the neighborhood,
makes you stand out. You do not belong here.
You do not fit in.

Gated

I was not at the party,
your anger is way out of place,
I had no part in it.
You can stay disappeared into your reality,
leave me out of it.

Rear View

I liked certain parts of it,
I cannot endorse it as a whole though;
therefore, it gets a negative review.
It is because of the people involved.
It is truly a case of prejudice.
It is worse because I used to like those involved—
I was fooled before,
I was stupid.

Leon

Are you just filled with regret
the next morning?
Does it all seem pointless?
Is there really nothing good that comes from it?
If that is an actual fact, nothing,
there really does need to be something done about it.

Shine

I'm talking, dancing, drinking, I'm socializing.
Everybody can do and say the exact same thing,
I'm somehow doing it not quite exactly,
in a good way.
And I know it.
And I can still function with this knowledge!
Amazing!

Occupation as an Artist

1973

Please, don't be like me,
don't blame this self-consciousness as the poison apple.
Now, I think it's just a lifestyle or something.

Easy Life

An illness,
drug use,
public shame,
something always gets in the way,
something always interferes.

Faded

I know I am on an artistic level, and I am not myself.
I wouldn't diagnose narcissism,
not yet.
I would test for amnesia though,
I think that happens quite a bit.
The night before simply didn't happen.
That, or some other milder form of disassociation.

Dissonance

The tricky part is getting clean voice samples.
Where they go at night, some of these people,
they are very exclusive,
sometimes,
if you know what I mean.
In the modern age, we have chat samples.
Studies can be made of them.

"Have these samples sent to the linguistics department stat,"
the samples being *Skype for Business*, *Kik*, and *eHarmony*, etc.
Having multiple chats at once,
different accounts on top of each other
simultaneously competing for the persons attention,
this yields very interesting responses.
There's still nothing like the voice though.

Sword

The minstrel follows the knight.
He is allowed to chronicle.
No one else is left alive.
No one else *can* say a word.

Decrease

Happy and contented
and a word just like *bigoted* that includes the entire world,
the disease has isolated itself,
in situ.

Disposition

Normal body functions will continue,
no treatment is indicated—
annual surveillance.
See you next year.

Mathers

I have done your genealogy.
It seems a large part of your grandmother lineage
broke down in their fifties,
froze up, crawled into bed,
and literally rotted away.
Are those your kids outside?
There were other causes of death.
The wealthier ones among them had doctors
come around once a week to monitor the horror,
prescribe an ointment.

Motive

Well, I did some research.
It turns out what I did was right.
You are the exact opposite of *feelings hurt*.
Feeling hurt means being sad even if just for a second.
Bullies are never, ever sad.

Spectacles

Triggered aggression,
if it can be,
is ignored.
All the books say so.
Human problems can be dealt with,
only afterward,
the same as always,
only afterward.

Silent Treatment

You can be around me and do your job.
You can ride the public transit with me,
and even sit next to me when it's crowded,
but do not speak with me
until I give you permission.

Mayfield

What's mostly left is a destitute population—
army run hospitals,
army run banks,
martial law.
No city wants you,
you're stuck.

Unrighteousness

An act of nature can hide incompetence.
"Okay, the emergency's over. Let's try that thing again."
But look at the numbers, the bottom line.
The numbers before that weren't because of an act of nature.

Thursday

What is it? Five years or so and you will be on your own,
divorced, kids off to Dartmouth or the University of Miami,
you will be able to write that novel you've been thinking of.
In the meantime, I will help you to get your mind right.

Hard Stop

Because it resembles a truth, a *real* criticism,
it demands a rigorous investigation,
and it demands a foregone conclusion,
that puts the council in an uncomfortable position.

Big Brother

It is the one true story.
The great big, stupid ape is in charge,
he has been elected dictator.
Everyone who agrees gets a job. Disagrees? Don't ask.
The story is this type of thing going on unabated for years,
graying,
then you have the novel.

Signed

It is a piece of earth donated by a local artist.
There is an explicit direction to do absolutely nothing.
He did say to have a dedication though,
have it filmed and everything,
after that, nothing.

Work

Morning park and ride,
morning bus,
evening park and ride,
home,
nothing ever changes.

Skype

I wish it was time to go.
These days are not passing by,
the calendar is heavy,
there is nothing to do,
and these people are making it worse.

Poster

His face is so terribly ordinary.
That's what makes it so ghastly.
A handsome man loses some of his humanity.
And he is not deformed,
you can't even find meanness—horrible.
This is in absolute contrast to the physical reality
of what is lived in,
you don't have to search for the horror there.

Nightfall

It went on for an eternity,
but summer seemed short this year.
Cool weather must have lingered into July,
everything else did.
It's definitely fall now,
it gets dark so soon.
It is surprising, welcome, and dreary all at once.

Going Good

I don't need to do anything,

at least for a while,
that is what I must keep in mind.
Anytime the thought, I must do this,
crosses into my mind,
I must resist myself.
Nothing needs to be done.

The Rat

It is becoming unbearable.
People are going outside to talk on the phone.

Kidding Ourselves

Are the younger ones the meaner ones,
the more aggressive?
They marginalize themselves, don't they,
in schools?
The other children don't cross them,
but there is no other respect.
Their intelligence is not respected at all.
In the adult world,
the older they get,
the weaker the prey,
then the younger ones come in—
I guess you are right.

World-Weary Eastside

There are definitely some prime pieces of lean meat out there,
ones that have boats,

property,
nice cars,
just got to do a little digging.

Treacherous

Try the new game from Hasbro!
Become the one who controls!
Denounce your opponents!
Read out loud the action cards!
Shout them directly in your opponent's face!
Over thirty varieties!
But beware!
Defeated opponents get unseen hands!
Those pieces are still on the board!
Land on them, and the special popomatic feature engages!
Pop! Back to square one!
Eventually one player gets the ace of spades!
And all other player are eliminated!
All at once!

Game Arrives

"Each game that ends actually goes on forever."
That is the message on the pink sheet of paper
which releases from the freshly opened box
and statically clings to my shirt.
The game board is made of two pieces.
The top part is made of burlap,
it has the design of the game, three concentric circles,
red, gold, and green,

with many glittering spaces dotting them geometrically.
The corners have snaps, real snaps,
you snap these onto the second part of the board.
This second part is electric.
It is standard game board size only thicker.
It has an obvious cavity inside.
Inside is where the popomatic stuff is, the magnets,
the slots for the game cards, the cards themselves,
the electrics, the circuitry.
There are fourteen decks of Mystery Cards.
Somehow all of these fit into the cavity.
That have to be shuffled and entered into a shoe
prior to the start of the game.

Game On

Each side of the gameboard has a slot for receiving
and sliding back in the game cards, mostly Mystery Cards,
but there are also Action Cards, and the ace of spades.
Each player has a visible game piece.
Each player also has an invisible game piece.
You have to remember where your invisible game piece is.
Each player also has a stylus.
In turn, the board ejects a game card,
usually a Mystery Card,
these contain how many spaces
to move your visible game piece.
Each card also gives you the option
to move your invisible game piece.
The rest of the card is in computer language,

it doesn't matter what it says.
You just get the card,
step off the visible game piece,
and indicate on the card with your stylus
what section you want
to move your invisible game piece to,
if any, then return the card.
You just leave the invisible game piece where it is
most of the time.
Most people pantomime signing the cards
to mask whether they are changing anything or not.
That is the spectacle, each person doing this in turn.
Every once in a while,
someone will stand up and denounce an opponent,
shouting all the expletives on the Action Card.
This happens about every five minutes.
The game usually lasts three hours.
When a player is denounced,
that person's visible game piece's tiny little head pops
and little bit of red liquid splatters,
and the player has to go back to square one
and get a new game piece,
there are thousands.
This also happens if you land on an unseen hand—
move the spaces on the Mystery Card and pop,
red liquid.
Unseen hands are created when you denounce an opponent.
They are invisible
and are devoted only to your destruction,
the one who denounced,

they are revenge.
This madness continues until someone gets the ace of spades,
pop,
pop,
pop.

Refund

I will ask for my money back.
Not many people ask for their money back.
I will make some kind of meaningless point
to a minimum wage computer operator somewhere.

Spoonie

You had more fun in one day back then
than I've had in my entire life.
There's a bit of disconnect there.

Alien Encounter

You are malnourished,
you are radioactive,
yes,
I hear you.
I am your hero,
I will come to your assistance,
and I will never speak of it again.

Ghost Encounter

Six grams per liter,
got it,
and I will receive a radiation suit tomorrow,
okay,
and I will bring it with me every day.
Only I can know—
and an air cast and brace,
right,
got it.

Human Contact

Rarely are they used.
They can be reached by phone.
It is just something they do, and then forget about.

Warning Message

Sometimes I drive.
I must turn off my phone when I drive.
There is an incident correlation.
I must not drive off cliffs.

Post Modem

You are a robot,
not cyborg anymore—
Universe Explorer 2425123,
Document 13321,
incendiary device, dormant,
incendiary device, dormant,

incendiary device, dormant,
incendiary device, open,
message,
unlimited credit all bank accounts.

Star Base Four

Only non-verbal communication is allowed.
Telepathy-Temporal is spoken here.
Andrew, you are the color blue.
As you enter the arena,
you are restricted to telekinesis as well.
Andrew, your number is 0.
We hope you have enjoyed your trip.
Private rooms are available to recuperate.
Andrew, your section is west.

Confirmation

I am a hero.
I will never speak of this.
I have made it into the database.
I am getting confused about the numbers.

Sophocles

I bring the hubris with me.
I've seen this before,
a hundred times.
The actor knows the script too.
We are on equal footing.

Protagonist

He just wants a Christian club,
perform marriage ceremonies,
minister at funerals,
and have meetings.
He absolutely does not want too many members.
Rarely gives out his card.

Drama

I am macho with a soft *a*.
Both men and women are satisfied in my presence.

Unspun

Totally dedicated agents are at work,
hypervigilant,
catching up on each ping,
adding little notes next to each finding.
They are slowly constructing the skeleton key
with the million ridges,
that's going to open up the door in your face.

Update

They are logging in to your lower offices,
your little friends,
your little secrets,
your little partners.

1973

Bad News

It's hot here, ninety.
What does air conditioning feel like
when you're about to be arrested?
The Pulse technology is in your cars,
in your homes.
Where are you right now?
Listen,
hear that faint technology?
It's audible.

Pulse

All the circulation turns inward,
line crews, so to speak,
protecting the infrastructure.

Repulse

Every time you convince yourself
that you are not going to be arrested,
that stops some of this potential inward.
You have so much self-control!

Look Outside

For some reason, Seattle gets so blue.
A good part of your brain sees summer.
Fresh, hot circulation wakes open the pores
on this hot, sunny day,
but your shoes are inside here,

and it's cool.
It's so cold, sweating is impossible—
panic is the correct thing to do!

Deep Layer

Do that other thing.
You should meditate or something.
Don't panic.
The only reason to panic has been dismissed.
It's hard to concentrate when you're shivering.
Not a shiver, a convulsion,
or a few—
but it's coming back,
hands and fists balled up and flailing,
contorting,
the baby crying, roaring—
for no reason!

It's All Contained

But you are shaking, you coward.
And it's not getting better.
No, you will not go out on the deck!
It is conscious now,
an objective physical manifestation,
it is conscious now,
things can be dealt with,
it is conscious now.

1973

I Am Safe

Take four-second breaths.
I am having a stroke.
Big pulse now, confusing the thoughts—
faint? What a coward!
Go outside.
Is ataxia a sign of a stroke?
That was just suggested! It can't be!
Deep, two-second, convulsant breaths.

I'm Outside

If something happens, you can just shout.
Don't!
No more suggestions!
As a learned man, you know passing out
is the best thing right now.
Flat out,
right here on the shaded deck,
you would be 100% recovered upon awakening.

Or Dead

How are you going to get out of this?
It is strengthening.
It has to be the four-second thing.
Keep doing that.
Think on the Buddha.
And all is right.
Even brothers and sisters are involved.

Arrest

Tell someone.
Have them call the cops on you,
it's worth the risk.
One person actively listening
and you actively talking
breaks up the maelstrom inside,
that thing that gets into your thinking.

Death

No,
tied up in a bag,
dirt,
dirt,
dirt.

Not Lovable

The whole thing together may be unpalatable,
but the excerpts are catchy
and readable,
not above,
below,
relatable.

Fan

He will give five stars.
He will give some critical remarks,
but end up saying

it's way better than anything else.

Context Equation

Something that isn't true,
not believed,
totally discounted,
can still get the feeling of truth
when synthesized with something else,
even if that something else is not believed in either, fiction.
The lie and the fiction mingle and create a weird truth.

Dramatic

All ka-ching aside,
there is a side of you that will suffer
when the Klieg light believers walk away.

Fanatic

There is nothing bad about it.
There cannot be a bad review.

Missed Note

It is the clanking kitchenware with me,
between the interesting stories,
the laughter,
all that jazz,
that in between time
when it's quiet and all I hear is the kitchenware,

that is when I know I don't belong.
No one is relating anything,
no one.
They can't possibly be waiting for me.

That Possibility

The crazy old coot that lives alone,
that sort of thing,
someone totally unrelatable to,
sneered at,
but this one's so cowardly
that he tries to be clever and friendly when confronted,
he doesn't even have the decency to bark,
to throw things.

That Sort of Subject

He can be examined.
A little VapoRub in the nostrils will do the trick.
I see someone who's lost his hair badly,
he has a strange u-shape,
I see someone who cannot smile.

Completely Apart

Walter Mitty in its most pathetic and comic sense.
Tragic too, but only while he lives,
not at the end.
When he drags his blood-shitting body to the county hospital,
absolutely no one will care.

1973

Prehistory

It crosses everyone's mind.
I would stop myself from being that way,
stop myself from believing that cult leader,
stop myself from being a junkie—
wouldn't let it get to fifty-five!

Edit

"Classic? El cheapo!"
This is part of the transcript of the audible dialogue
on the surveillance footage of the subject.
He was watching a television commercial
for an economy brand of toilet paper.
That was his comment.
He was all by himself.

Ego Sadness

Being rejected on *American Idol Audition*,
and then it's televised,
that can take up to about 20% of yourself.
Sometimes the 80% can throw itself
into the most dramatic of melancholies.

Verbal Assault

My ventricles burst out between my ribs,
my eyes look for some hidden truth.
I become out of body.
Maybe one day I will turn around,

take my breath slow,
stand still,
lift up my chin,
and smile.

Careful

I would get on that busy street that heads toward the freeway.
I would cross this street, and then the next one.
I would watch for all the lights,
and the pedestrians.
I would try to be wary of all the cars around me.

Idiot-Proof

Hazards between the blowers,
fix-a-flat instead of spare,
don't worry,
the car is brand new—
and all the sensors everywhere.

Bemused Horror

It's really rarely seen.
It probably looked similar with the nobility in 1789,
continuing to perpetuate an idea that has been rejected.
Although now, right has become righteous.

Tavern

This is exactly the opposite of what I thought.

Thought is not the right word, made up.
The stools, the floor, the amps, it's all terrible.

Incult

Future generations, we did not think
that Geico commercial was funny.
We may take a hit for being cowardly,
and not standing up to abject ignorance,
but don't knock our taste.

Guilt

Getting past it usually takes a very short time.
It always crosses my mind that it will linger.
That is an extremely unpleasant thought.
So, it becomes nothing?
It does go away. It doesn't become nothing, that would be
a delusion.
It is buried and haunts.

Love

I attract human traffickers and cults.
It is a brainy sort of thing though.
I find it very attractive.
You get to like what you inspire.
I can't go by the normal route. There has to be
lawyers on retainer, contracts ready to be signed,
controlled substances, and religion.

Handler

I see him in the van.
I see him at the outside table.
There he is again.

Bad Spirits

Thousands of houses
and quiet
and darkness.
Good news, and a firecracker goes off, yay!
Someone else heard it, another firecracker.
Finally, a third.
A few hours later, bad news, a firecracker goes off, boo,
someone is ill.

The Future

You lend in a crisis.
You will always have something coming in
after.
And the ones who pay are the ones to be close to
after.

Scrolls

The little idols please the gods.
They are collected to please them.
Another and another, as fast as they can be produced.
People are poisoned who do not buy,
cursed.

There would have to be a lot of them,
in revolt or destitute,
to smash the idol makers.
Then there will be books to be read.
Collect those.

A Place of Empty People

Tinny broadcasts are heard, echoing through the trees
and backyards,
like a voice singular,
speaking and then cheers.

Grades

Things aren't believed in as much as they used to be,
the strong evidence,
the loud voices,
aside.
Everything today is an attempt to *be* history,
to get an A,
F is for forgotten.

In Your Depression Circle

I'm sorry, I'm not in your pressure gradient.
Your depression whirlpool can just wind
itself into its nothingness
without me.
You can express your mass hysteria,
float around in your dread,

moan out your kumbayas
alone.

Benefit

It's kind of a trick then, isn't it?
A small outlay of cash for a lifetime of volunteerism?
It's not a very good trick.

Advocate

I think I can realize when I am being taken advantage of,
I don't need you to tell me.
I care,
I don't need you to care for me.

Opinion

The Department of Propaganda has gone on strike,
and the ticker has gone blank.

Cruel Summer Day

Cool morning and the windows are opened,
it is fully dawn,
and there is the smell of sunscreen.

Underwriter

Another disaster!
What is happening?
Take charge!

Who is in charge of this section?
Have a meeting!
A take no prisoners type of meeting!

Escaped

Near death experiences are forgotten by animals.
Remember it? Those flocks of birds go extinct.
The ones that forget about what the cat just did
go on.
The next worm has to be eaten,
the next whatever.

Animal Kingdom

The blue jay hadn't seen one,
a human,
hadn't smelled one.
And this one has strong colors,
and instinct—
I don't like the way this one is eyeballing me, Jim.

Wigs

We have people in your firms.
They are not spies per se,
they are just being honest.
They are bookkeepers, accountants,
things like that.
You have created these little geniuses.
They are lung cancer.

Softer

The 1950's loudspeakers,
they are so far away,
do you hear them?
Another recorded performance.
That is the children's camp, I think.

Fringe

Stupidity as a people
must have a source.
People all on board doing something
that has the opposite effect
intended,
they must have a completely skewed perception of reality
because they keep doing it.

Pens

It will be bloody,
it will be torture,
that will be the fall.
What a terrible thing,
positioned
as you wished others.

Ruled

Hated after loved,
that mix unleashes.
But always loved,

the hate has to be invented.
It is searched for,
it is acted on,
it is sung about,
and it is
always,
disappointing.
It is pretend.

Hid

When it is overt in the playground,
you can see it in the victim.
Out of body,
that is the way to go,
it can't stay here.

The Alternative

When something is truly successful,
there is no turning back.
You've gone through the door.
There is a new normal that can only be avoided
by ignoring it.
I want you to watch that money,
don't wish it would stop,
you might as well go all the way.
There won't be any drag from it,
just units accumulating,
numbers,
more and more.

Find outlets for it,
have that be your focus.
Accept your multimillion dollar income,
accept your position in the world—
purchases,
holdings,
cash.

The Lie

It's always the thing a little bit further.
There's always a surprising person too,
someone to guide you through the wilderness,
to lead you to the wholly wrong place.
That is the thing you must be very careful of.

Damn These Times

I cannot let my ego choose things.
When it gets gratified (you'd think I would know),
it can change the makeup,
and I will not know what to do.

The Joker

He comes out and dances among the ruins.
That is cool?
That is a performance?
I will show you one…

The Ruins

1973

I deny the implication of totalitarianism,
there is no great thinking behind it.
It is obviously just cowardice,
and letting stupid people bully.
I will look at what's really going on.
Let the swine believe what they want,
I won't be able to convince most of them anyway,
the imbeciles.

Back to Jack

To the fool currently dancing,
you have a handsome enough face,
you can perform,
you qualify,
you listen to a Seal song,
get a little crazy,
and perform.
And there you have it—
brilliant?

Creepy Influence

I guess it would go from the aborted fetus vaccines
to the Soylent Green analogy,
to *1984*.
I will stick with the pathetic organization
that destroys itself entirely.

They Asked Us

What's more than a million?
And more than a billion?
And a trillion?
The last was a zillion.
That was the progression.
This sign,
billion, trillion, zillion,
it was put up the first day,
and it stayed up the entire year—
like six hours a day,
five days a week
for nine straight months.
Not reminded of a mistake every day,
for we all knew,
but advised to a mistake generally,
subliminally—
please do this,
progress this way,
dance the mistake all over convention,
unleash the creative side.
"This will be our sign, our motto."
And then nothing ever again.
People told her about quadrillion,
but just two words were wasted on it,
and it was dismissed.

Order of Things

Satan is not smarter than me.
Could he fool me into thinking I'm defeating him

without hardly doing a thing?
And is he so crafty as to have me take some credit for it?
Not being in the same league as Job,
I would be being obliterated like a bug
just for ludicrous kicks,
I guess.
There would not be a negotiation to oppress.
That's not helping to justify his intelligence.
From my point of view, it is just pure evil with no reason,
not even a high.
From the species' point of view, a horror show
staged out supernaturally everywhere and all at once,
without even individual attention.
Ignorant and oblivious is comedy,
and tragedy,
and stupidity.

Clear Thinking

Let's see,
the charge was that I am
an ignorant and oblivious fool
being fooled by a much more intelligent adversary.
I think I have reasoned that,
in actuality,
I would be just be mimicking the imbecile
in ignorance and oblivion if I believed that.
I will continue winning instead.

Striking

Would it be Britain?
The slight differences are appealing.
And they are watching the whole drama.
I'm not.

Audience

What does that make me? The entertainer.
Everybody else repeating a drivel
sets off an inspiration even more—
everybody!
Mine's striking and unique,
mine's a different message,
the truth,
and it needs to be bought.

Innocence

And the lack of 24/7 comes off as ignoring too,
it's marvelous!

Calm Down

People are clever,
people are afraid.
Clever is relaxed,
afraid is paranoid.
Paranoid can sound clever,
but it puffs itself out,
and the rest is interminable.
It's not that it will not end,

it's that it cannot end.

I Quit!

A sudden break has its advantages too.
And sometimes it's the appropriate thing to do.
The craving for the drug
in the former addict
is the strongest at the first minute,
and then it winds down.
It's the same principle with unemployment.
This is especially true
considering it has to be new employment,
being forced out and all.

Sales

Calculated sums at zero,
in comparison to an existent thing, the opposite,
just potential,
and only potential because I'm writing about it,
other than that, nothing.

Act One, Scene One

This one has a heavy presence on the stage.
He has to be the first to speak,
alone.
It has to be an apology almost
before the carnage begins.

Richard

This is what I did,
I set my brothers against each other quite on purpose,
but also quite subconsciously—
I was possessed.
I did this because I am ugly,
and I can't abide in courtly peace.
How I proceed from thence shouldn't be a surprise then,
should it?
I am the aggressive one.
No one,
not even Edward is in my league.
As a knight,
everyone is at my mercy.
I have a trained animal fearless underneath me.

Saul

That is what they had to do,
prepare a special place,
it had to be built.
"It will serve its purpose, and then be burned,
the place to repair the veil."
No one knew the weight of the thing.
They were all invited to the holding area,
the scribes and mathematicians,
to the special place,
the same place where all the slaves lived.
Some were left off the list because of Samaritanism.
After the lambs were slaughtered,

all the lambs,
they were let in one by one,
the unclean minds.
Lastly, they let in the taskmaster.
All were let in to come up with a figure,
the least amount of men to move the holy relic.
Also the technique,
how to lay it correctly with no feet touching it,
no elbows,
and how to space out the weavers, the thread,
again the least amount possible.
"Once the logistics, you see, are worked out,
you just await the fullness of time,
amen."
It took 24 times.
It took that many times
before the thing was even moved to the holding area—
and that wasn't done right.
The step of laying out correctly took 50 times,
and that took more men than moving it.
We all know the happy ending,
it was mended, enough thread was found,
but it took years.
That is the image I want to bring before you,
the years.
How quickly it was all built up,
and how eagerly expanded.
The tents,
the bleating,
the slaughter—

for three years.
And the stench—
holy!
Every single biceps, quadriceps, eyeball had to be cleansed
before going in.
"Trespassing! Put an end to it!"
The slaughter put a gaze on them,
a hunger to find the next yearling.
But we who had to pass by it each day
to vote,
to allocate,
to uproar and quiet,
we had to be efficient,
we had to pass through it stiff with tears in our eyes.
But beyond the walls we were seen,
and it spread.

Ergo

They would actually do that as they tried to escape,
"Let me go, or I will cut the boy's throat!"
And then they would!
And then they themselves would die.
These maniac's deaths,
one after another,
or rather, two after another,
clouded the minds of those who had to witness it,
it stained their minds.

Scape

1973

What is deemed worthwhile?
What I am not, young and all left to live—
at last, a truth,
"That is what I present before you,"
and it was always a little boy.
Some flashed on the ancient religion,
became instant converts to paganism
in their last minute.
Everlasting life, paradise,
they became the opposite of their dogma after all.
These stories are so sad,
And it's sad to everyone.
We see ourselves potentially.
But in the man himself,
in that person there is no sadness,
he is panicked,
afraid,
and natural.
He occupies *that* space in your mind,
he has that potential,
that consciousness—
read it in a few lines at the top,
then skip down to the bottom,
yep,
he did it.

Sold Himself Out

The garrisons see this,
they skip down to the bottom in their own way,

contemplatively detailing everything.

Hacks

I don't believe it is a real phenomenon,
it is bigfoot, ancient aliens.
These eyewitnesses aren't describing actual things.
These poets aren't experiencing real feelings.
Their outrage is in a very logical part of the brain,
not in the emotions!
It is a misidentification, as Ranae would say.

Hero Speech

So it never even gets the second dimension,
it is enclosed in the logical center of the mind,
mimicking an emotion,
and thus barring any interaction with real feelings.
They do have the third dimension of experience—
do they ever!
But it cannot do anything,
the memory,
it remains only a potential,
if logic and emotion haven't linked up.

Sacrifice

When organizations break down,
they start to sell each other out.
"What's worthwhile? My colleague, here. I will kill him."
And he does!

1973

Secret Agent

Disconnect the battery, disconnect the computer system,
get the bleach,
get the van here,
activate everything!

Starving

I can't believe I won't contact people!
I know it takes me a while to get to know people,
and I'm an old goat,
no one wants to get to know me to begin with,
but I wouldn't be alone!

Reflexive

This isn't some costumed nothing,
these are people you know,
these are people that will hurt you,
they are alive, not history,
in your face,
"Where's Anne Frank?"
And you will tell them
in a second.

My Business

I do have dreams sometimes,
being in that backyard,
and that kitchen light being on,
and that long driveway,

those green trees—
it's late, it's quiet, and I am about.
I'm in someone's backyard,
my neighbor's,
I want to know what's going on in there,
in that house.
I am not supposed to know.
It's always cold and quiet,
and that light is on.
A late dinnertime?
I don't think anyone's home.
The front is very dark,
there is no porch light even on,
just the gray streetlight
barely.
There is stairs leading up to that back light,
and an outside light too—
those stairs could be tricky in the dark.

Arterial

There were other houses that had weird architecture,
at least to me,
zig-zagging stairs in the front,
up to the second level—
and this facing a major street.
But that was the back, I think,
the rest faced a nice view of the valley,
and the mountains,
probably beautiful.

1973

Rear

But back here,
in the dream,
this backyard is unkempt,
just like mine,
just like yours,
natural.

Alley

There was also an alley I visited in my sleep.
I always felt like a trespasser there too—
but it's an alley!
The alley dreams would be like on Halloween,
after it's all done,
whatever o'clock,
bullies in the neighborhood,
going through the city.
Get home quick, take the alley.
The night has a smell of frozen mold,
and a sound like quiet walking.
I am always looking to steal something
in the alley dreams,
and there are always people there,
in the trash,
in the garbage,
doing things,
alien things,
doing something with cord or wire,
filling cans up,

moving dirt,
piling something.
I come upon them quite suddenly,
the light and angles are that way,
I hear them first,
then they are illuminated,
their backyard, their look, my look back—
then the next backyard.
Those are the alley dreams.

Not My Business

Late at night, in other dreams,
I visit where the general stores were,
the bar,
the laundromat,
the pharmacy,
I wake up there in the middle of the night—
come on, in the middle of the night!
It's like four AM!
It is absolutely dead.
I am going home the fast way,
and regretting it.
So much grass this way,
black, dark grass and foot breadths—
a wrong turn here, and a dead end.
I should know this, this is my neighborhood!
But no, a wrong turn, and a backtrack—
and now
I am

completely lost.
I am on Lake Drive somehow,
and I am starting to run into people—
cue waking up in a sweat.

Aurora

Also,
in other dreams,
staying on the bus too long,
in the middle of the night,
heading towards downtown,
crossing that bridge,
last stop for a while,
last bus for a while,
ending up at Seattle Center—
God, up there in the middle of the night!

Corner Lots

And then there were the really big houses.
It always seemed like no one lived in those.

Lot's Corner

He had to have observed some things,
the six-foot angels in front of him,
for example.
Also, the blindness,
but this was between God and the cities.
If he hustled out too quickly, that would be endorsing,

a sign of interference—
it doesn't matter what he thinks.
Advocation, encouragement?
His mind was always on the bottom line,
his business,
not on the mountains.
The next city,
getting things going after,
keeping things going,
that's where his head was at.

Intermission

I think I have a bit of a fever,
my brain should be coming up with some good dreams.
It's not.
I don't feel bad. Had that scratchy throat,
but it never developed into anything.
I've had a few migraine-related things, flare ups.
No congestion.
Abdominally, things aren't perfect,
but nothing *sickness* would describe.
It's most likely some kind of hormonal thing,
an enzyme imbalance.
The captain will adjust things.

Blokes

The end of the internet,
where the tumbleweeds go,
old stuff,

dead poets with still alive bank accounts,
their stuff,
there are still offerings for it back here.
The dead's brother takes ownership of the account,
and intends to look at it
someday.
Until then, it still gets shown in places like here.

UK

This place should have a French name,
a place with *-iers* at the end,
a place that speaks English.
Maybe some place in Ireland,
that would be nice.
Everything's so anonymous.

Macs

I have to get in the lorry and drive way out where?
God's eyes, I deserve a raise.
And just this little package,
this little book.
What a life,
sticking it in some rural box.

Guile Necessary

I just want the shades of gray sweaters
to hear something different for once,
not hear what they can mimic,

nor be furnished, then stripped.
I am not in the logical,
I am not in your vocabulary muscles,
I'm stuck in your reflex,
not quite up to the brain pan.

Rusty Pop Machine

Kindle E-reader,
KDP Select plus Expanded Distribution,
that is what brought me to this site.
An IV needle,
and slowing bleeding out bank account,
that is what keeps me here.

Hit

Just picking up a freebie or half-price thing.
Amazon Prime member,
got the e-book right away,
get the artifact soon.

The Problem

What a spectacle.
Is this what they think happiness is all about?
Is this what the doctors think?
Create your own rituals,
deaths,
weddings,
births,

get ideas from the communities,
visit houses,
visit friends!
It can give the appearance of beauty,
be absolutely perfect,
intricate,
but don't you have to keep doing it?

Distributors

It's not really true,
they make their money,
they earn it too.
"$2.99, what a bargain. I have a Kindle."
They get a click,
Amazon rewards them.
It's all unleashed,
it's all in the circuitry,
the binary logic,
2020—
revenue streams going every which way.
A few developers made up this grand scheme,
and improved upon it,
and improved upon it,
now it's the free flow and interchange of ideas,
paid ideas,
and I am getting a big piece of it.

Civilian

I'm from the justification side of Christianity.

I believe man is in a natural state of sin.
The only possibility is pardon,
and that is faith.
It seems short and easy,
an Easter egg if you can find it,
a hack.
But the 100% faith that's asked for
is a martyr kind of love,
a mentally unbalanced one,
no one has it.
We all have a kernel,
and it works pretty well for the past and the future,
but as a living thing,
everyone is lacking.

Bodhi

Be introspective,
see the self-righteousness,
know the thoughts,
sit under the doubtful, ancient tree.

Season of the Witch

The device is flashing green,
kind of flesh toned,
and neon green,
with enigmatic little messages flying by,
unnoticed.
"Happy, happy Halloween, Halloween, Halloween.
Happy, happy Halloween, Silver Shamrock."

1973

The hypnotism
produced by the machine,
spectacles capture it in an image.

Target Audience

My book,
right in your face,
and it flashes,
and it flashes again,
it is scoring your face,
preparing it for the skin graft.
Are you the correct population?
Not yet?
You are prepared, though, when the time comes—
millions of Shadys.

Spooky

Let's see if this gets through.
All my good thoughts, my fantasies
(I want good things, I deserve them),
all these things I am communicating to you,
and you are understanding every word of it.
Dealing in high-value currency here,
not ESP.

Is That So?

I can receive ESP just fine,
but this is not invisible stuff,

what I am sending,
these are words,
lyrics,
images,
experienced *things*.

Connection

I think about this all the time,
even during work,
dinners,
all the time.
You're welcome.

Conductor

Let me show you this.
"I believe that."
Listen to this.
"I believe that."
It is an awesome power.

Converts

The cooler it is, the more successful,
and the more lumbering,
the competition.

Extroverts

Superstars have to soak themselves into it, don't they?

To keep the dynamic honest,
even if it's in secret,
I think they do.

Introverts

If I had a lumbering product,
I would be ashamed.

History Book

Maybe it was a chat group,
and this was just picked it at random
for real criticism,
discussion.
"Everything you get is not good, you know."
That is the bottom line, the purpose of this exercise.
Instead,
it's all of them,
not half not understanding it, or thinking it's bad,
all of them blown away by it.
"Good." "Good." "This is really good."
Then the leftists come in and shit all over it.

Nephilim

I am effective in that way too.
They lose a lot of respect.
They seem really *banny* and *hashtaggy*.
They seem thick too.

Waterfall

And they keep coming,
another book,
another book,
another book,
not deteriorating,
getting better,
relentless.

Fifteen or Sixteen

So ugly, so repulsive,
that brings the abnormal self-view.
It will be a lot of things, but not the truth.
It is a disorder because it's so total.
There is nothing left of the germinal.

The Germinal

There were flashes in the back
and flashes forward,
but around that time,
this man simply had to go—
don't even try.

New Man

Probably end up being pathological.
Most likely failed, not a headliner,
just out there in the private investigator's files,
and police would have made inquiries.

1973

New Things

No, it will not happen.
I don't want to.
I don't want to be a part of it.
I don't want to learn new things.
Hobbies?
It's what it leads to!

Old Things

Things have evened out with age.
The old have been clouded.
They don't age well,
most of them.
And they best not bring their weak shit up on me,
I will fill up their grills with the Holy Ghost.

The Medium

There would be reviews.
It seems that is what a lot of people are put on this world for.
A marketed book gets that reaction,
not mine.
Weird creatures start reading mine,
isolated,
and ready to start something cool.

Literati

People that write too much get *writey*.
They write to be understood, but only by a few.

When things need to be explained to others, they aren't.
The secret handshake comes out, and we are excluded.

Cold Wind

It is a vital piece of information.
It enters the tongue.
Although quite busy,
"Oh, it's cold,"
spreads the news.

Donated Books

It goes into the recycle bin,
it flows from there,
and ends up in the homeless' hands.
It is good.
Important truths are learned.
It goes into the therapist's hands,
and then onto the shelf,
and then into the poet/addict's hands,
your hands.

Fooled You

My acting performance was memory and emotion.
They mixed together a little, those two different things.
The dialogue, a single finite unit, it just flowed out.

Read

They want your books to examine.
They want to know your contacts.
Who were you in high school?
Prep school?
Oh my god, we have to look into that!

Morality Wealth

Talk about covetousness!
All the charities!
The causes!
Look at what I do!

Seven-Letter Word

The *I am good* statement can never be true,
but it sits in there all the time,
on the tip of your tongue,
in the way.

Start Up

I've convinced myself it's a good business.
I will work hard to make it successful—
me successful!
Yes, I will be part of the community.
Sustainability, equality, generosity,
that is what I will be known for,
and standing up against oppression,
and being ready for and responding to disasters,
and volunteering.

Bankruptcy

I've been tricked somehow,
it's just a money pit.
I am the all-time sucker.

Bankruptcy Court

My life is a film.
No one is in the theater.
It is the closing credits.
I am scored.
I am alone.

Psi-War

People are just avoiding the violence.
This has been a total miscalculation.
What is the solution?
Second verse same as the first,
provoking the enemy into an atrocity,
or into saying the wrong thing—lol,
it never ends.

Shop

That sort of thing won't sell.
I get the illusion of it,
a sip.
It gives me a reason to pay another month's rent
as the sales dribble in.
Sucker.

I make everything a little bit cheaper for everyone else,
the super users,
the successful artists with the savvy marketing strategies.

Royalty

Our perfumed heroes will have something to say,
and some of it will be interesting,
clever,
but none of it is ever real,
singular,
and neither are you,
you will be totally forgotten when passed away.

Discounts

The distributor is actually selling it for a price
that people might actually buy it for,
and they are offering it in a place
where people might actually pick it up.

Accounts

The idea is to make it a topic of discussion,
that is what is hoped for.
The kids say *relevant* because it's interesting,
but that somehow demeans it.

Counts

I think it's supposed to be

someone goes home and I totally pluck their beats.

Author's Page

I arrived in this colony in 1965.
I got to know everybody here quite well.
There was some kind of hypoxia
or something
going on in my brain.
I became very delirious at times.
I liked everyone's stories the best,
when they came around,
their fiction was very strong.
I tried a little of that in my convalescence.
I also did a little painting as well.

$9.99

A fair price,
that shouldn't even be thought of on my end.
When I start monkeying around
on the distribution end of things,
the creative flow to make things as good as possible
suffers.
The people whom I'm concerned with don't consider
the usual.

The Cloud

There are only a few out here.
If you don't have a good carrier,

you won't get a signal.

Viral

Sterno and crying in *The Andromeda Strain*,
surviving in Seattle.

Thinking

In the way, coming to me, approaching,
that's one group.
And those who slipped away and stayed away,
it takes an effort to remember them,
but that's the other group.
A few of the latter may understand.

Footnote

Saying it can't be a judgment on a city
without it being Armageddon
is not right.

Bessie

It can't be anything good,
or rarely so.
I am a cow.

All

A big part of it is that everybody sees it.
That is the coexisting reality.

The messiah complex
and
that everybody sees it.
That makes it grow.
And it feeds, it hunts.

More

Even accidental utterances
made by some unknown person,
made forty years ago,
is devoured.
Every single thing in existence,
that is what it has become.

Then Nothing

Now,
ignore this reality,
maybe on the job or whatever,
interact with people on that continuum—
I'm normal, you're normal.
What can be their reaction to that?

Now Back

Then,
you go back to and do it again,
full glory,
unmistakable,
a halo and a radiant light—

what then?

Strangeways

It does make you want to lose.
That's not a good way of putting it,
but the fact that it actually happens that way
constantly
cements that *losing* thing in the mind.
It is more that you want something going in,
something better,
replacing.

Used

If someone comes in and pays your bills for you,
they are not doing it for you,
they are doing it for themselves.

Ogre

You are an uneducated lowlife,
an ugly remnant of the uncircumcised.
You're completely outside of society,
living under bridges,
hurting children.

Regime

It's like hearing Saddam Hussein died or something,
overthrown

finally,
and then seeing him in the flesh,
inspecting your neighborhood,
asking,
"Who has complaints? I hear there are complaints.
I want to hear them. Tell them to me."

Down in the Park

I have been guided into a successful marriage.
I have five healthy kids.
I was mentored through a world-class education.
I am an executive now.
I have a high position within the party.
I may even lead it one day.
I am sitting in the park, eating my sandwich.
I chew it many times.
My glasses fog as I breathe through my nose.
I swallow awkwardly.

Assignment

We have to convince him of something,
something that isn't true.
Make him defend himself,
make a joke of it,
say something.
If he goes on and purchases something,
something to make up for it,
then he's firmly in our grasp.
The next step is to have somebody come in

and correct that error,
you.

Something Missing

I have to purchase things.
I don't have to purchase things.
What else is there to do?

David Joshua

My body rebels against it,
and then my mind…
I can't go wrong!
No wild untruth!
Assassinations,
witchcraft,
cults,
organized crime—
it is a body.
I am confronted,
it cannot be beaten—
but I have music,
I have the stones,
I am the one who defeats it.

Evil

Whatever it is, it won't be well thought out.
It will be to just do evil, nothing else.
The only reason it seems clever is because it works.

It must be clever, right?

Artifact

It was burned,
and then it rained.
Everything flooded,
every piece of debris
was scattered everywhere,
and it blended in with the ground.

Opinion?

My mind purposely hides from thing it knows.
It says it doesn't know for sure, that's the first step.
Then it's not my place.
These two things kind of jostle back and forth,
they kind of contradict each other.
Then it fades.

Purpose

Then the cat is born.
I walk slowly
as fast as I can.

Old Polished Malls

A lot of very simple people,
young people,
way over there with the heavy feet,

they know what to buy.
They know they don't have anything
right now,
but they will,
and they know just what to buy.

Myopia

You walked this way before,
now it's burned,
and you run.
You couldn't imagine anyone
with sense
disagreeing with you,
but now you are an oppressor.

Contained

Veiled and covered, only eyes,
a nose is prominent,
and silence.

Effective Sentences

This I find highly offensive.
This hurts my feelings.
The only way to defend against it
is to say, "I don't give a shit."
But that looks bad,
and it has untruth behind it,
because you really do care,

so it sounds bad too, unconvincing.
I wish I could fill in the *blanks*
of some more effective cry back,
but that is a losing game.
You have to kind of admit you do care,
and when you do that, you're finished.
The disingenuous denial ends the logical argument,
and the expletive in the response reinforces the ending.

To Get What They Want

It's crazy, why should it be surprising though?
Ruthless people come from powerful people,
and powerful comes from more powerful,
each is an end result in themselves.
The prime mover is evil.

Adults

We look for signs of lies,
that is sinful.
We have too high an expectation
that things are untrue.
We look forward to a time
when this is no longer the case,
but it can only be found when we were children.

Tuned

I did it for psychotic reasons at first.
When stabilized, I kept it going.

1973

Not sure why.
For continuation reasons?
There was also the reason of shutting out the real world.
Not really to not see things,
but to keep seeing things,
the things I used to see,
to keep being reminded of them in a small way,
to not let them get washed away,
forgotten.
It was a crazy success,
it's good to be reminded of a success.
Not blinkers,
smiley face tattoos on the inside of my eyelids.
That was me humming the old tunes,
drumming my teeth to them.
I used to do this for hours on end,
vacuuming office buildings,
cleaning bathrooms,
walking to the bus stop,
riding the bus.
The same song each night, over and over.
And tomorrow the next song,
the next letter in the alphabet.
And not the whole song, just the gist of it.
I guess if it was a simple song,
I would have the whole gist,
but if complex, it would be just partial.
Sometimes I mashed together two similar songs
by the same artist,
I don't know—

I didn't listen to much radio at the time.
This went on all day long when I was in public.
And this went on for almost twenty years.
It would disappear, of course,
in the customer service aspect of the job,
and with friends,
but this was the baseline, the idling speed.
Now I work on a computer terminal in my home office
all by myself,
and I listen to the actual songs
all day long,
surrounded by it,
headphones.
The inside of my brain greets this as an old friend,
Look at you! Look at you! You look great! Look at you!
It used to be all imagination and memory,
imagination and memory go out and greet it.

www.ingramcontent.com/pod-product-compliance
Lightning Source LLC
Chambersburg PA
CBHW070955080526
44587CB00015B/2313